Level 2.

REMEDIAL READING

LEVEL 2 TEACHER'S GUIDE

Holt, Rinehart and Winston, Inc.
New York Toronto London Sydney

Bill Martin's INSTANT READERS

TEACHER'S GUIDE LEVEL 2

by Bill Martin Jr.
and Peggy Brogan

Printed in the United States of America • ISBN 0-03-086201-9

CONTENTS

INTRODUCTION

Letter from Bill Martin Jr. 8

PART 1

Rationale of the InstantReader Program

On the very first day of the first grade, every child should have a book that he can joyfully read from cover to cover 12

The first and most basic reading skill is the belief, "I can read a book" 13

Book experience should precede word experience in bringing a child to print 14

A child has continuing need for whole book success throughout his reading career 15

An emerging reader needs a battery of books that he can zoom through with joyous familiarity 16

Young readers need the thrust of literary fellowship 18

Dramatic cumulative repetitions of language help children anticipate (and thereby decode) the printed page 20

Language skills are best learned in the shape and swing of a sentence 22

Dependable schemes of rhyme and rhythm help children read words they didn't know they knew 24

Emerging readers find quick success with stories that are patterned on familiar cultural sequences 26

Remedial reading should begin with every child role-playing himself as a successful reader of books 28

When a book involves a child Esthetically its message has more meaning 30

PART 2

Discussion of each title in the series

Whistle, Mary, Whistle 34

A Spooky Story 38

City Song 42

Old Mother Middle-Muddle 46

(continued)

(continued)

The Longest Journey in the World 50

King of the Mountain 54

Old Devil Wind 58

The Little Disaster 64

Tatty Mae and Catty Mae 68

I'm Going to Build a Supermarket One of These Days 71

PART 3

Follow-up activities for Level 2 books

Reading joyfully from cover to cover 76

Innovating on literary structure 77

Analyzing literary structure 79

Analyzing rhythmical structure 85

Analyzing sentence structure 86

Analyzing word structure 90

Responding to typographical intrigue 92

Responding to art 94

INSTANT READERS

LEVEL 2 Teacher's Guide

Letter from Bill Martin Jr.

INTRODUCTION

Dear friends,

The *InstantReaders* are an integral part
of the Bill Martin language-literature offerings
and therefore embody the basic philosophy
already spelled out in the *Sounds of Language* readers
and in the *Owl Books*.
The *InstantReaders*, however, especially focus
in new exciting ways
on the use of structure as a decoding skill
and the use of dependably structured books
in releasing children immediately to visions of themselves
as successful-and-pleasured readers.
It is this cover-to-cover immediacy,
along with esthetic and linguistic intrigue,
that makes the *InstantReaders* uniquely impressive
in a child's reading career.
No matter what kinds of reading materials
you are using in your classroom,
these books will add their own special dimensions by

1) instilling children with the belief that they can read
and at the same time providing them with materials
that support that belief,
2) cultivating joyous familiarity with a corps of language models
and book experiences
that serve as a leavening to skill acquisition,
3) incorporating sensitivities to structure
(rhyme, rhythm, phrase-sentence-and-story patterns)
for purposes of decoding,
4) capitalizing upon familiar linguistic and cultural structures
in launching children into reading,
5) involving children esthetically (as well as intellectually)
in the printed page,
6) holding wholebook*success* as a basic purpose
of reading instruction.

Three levels of InstantReaders

Level 1

Brown Bear, Brown Bear, What Do You See?
When It Rains, It Rains
A Ghost Story
The Haunted House
Silly Goose and the Holidays
I Went to the Market
Fire! Fire! Said Mrs. McGuire
The Wizard
Monday, Monday, I Like Monday
Up and Down the Escalator

Level 2

Whistle, Mary, Whistle
A Spooky Story
City Song
Old Mother Middle-Muddle
The Longest Journey in the World
King of the Mountain
Old Devil Wind
The Little Disaster
Tatty Mae and Catty Mae
I'm Going to Build a Supermarket One of These Days

Level 3

Ten Little Squirrels
"Tricks or Treats?"
Welcome Home, Henry
The Maestro Plays
The Happy Hippopotami
My Days are Made of Butterflies
What to Say and When to Say It
The Turning of the Year
I Paint the Joy of a Flower
The Eagle Has Landed

INSTANT READERS

LEVEL 2 Teacher's Guide

Rationale of the InstantReader Program

PART 1

the very

FIRST

DAY

of 1

grade,
every child
should have a book
that he can
joyfully read
from cover
to·cover

Children in our society inherit the need to read. They also inherit the expectancy that they will read a book the first day of first grade. When they don't, they go home disappointed—and the first breach between a child and reading success has been created.

How much better to invite those "first-dayers" to hear a highly structured book that they immediately can "read back" cover-to-cover. *Children, isn't this wonderful! Here it is only the first day of first grade and already you can read a book!*

The *InstantReader* program is designed to fulfill this cultural need for you and children. The *InstantReaders* are reading readiness at its best. They put a flow of language in children's ears and eyes and mouth, and fill their lives with the radiance of reading success.

THE FIRST and most basic *reading skill is the belief,* "I can read a book"

Over the years teachers, lacking surefire beginning books, have been forced to engage children in all sorts of reading readiness materials that have no connection whatsoever with a book, and sometimes even less with language. Consequently, children have been denied for six or more weeks fulfillment of their strong urge to read a book. Since six weeks can be a long time in a young child's life, all too many begin their reading careers by losing the urge to read and even by becoming confused about the act of reading. *Children, would you like to read another book today? Here it is only the second day of first grade and already you can read two books!* What better way to insure the reading success of a child than to send him home proudly declaring, *I can read! I can read!* This pervasive belief in himself as a reader is the underlying skill for his acquisition of all other reading skills.

The book is a cultural symbol of man's becoming. Our lives are shot through with evidence of this phenomenon: when we are cut off from book *success*, we feel less than worthy; to the contrary, we feel pleasured and proud having books around the house; we are more pleased with children when they spend time with books than when they spend time with TV; we brag to each other about the books we have read and are going to read; *etc*.

BOOK EXPERIENCE *should precede* WORD EXPERIENCE *in bringing a child to print*

Unfortunately, traditional reading instruction has never given wholebook*success* its proper emphasis. Rather it has set up an endless succession of hurdles, largely word oriented, that children must master, with very little concern for wholebook*success*. The *InstantReader* program, by contrast, provides wholebook*success* concomitantly with reading instruction. It makes the reading of entire books initially available to children through the ear, and gives them the constant support of the book symbol and its aura of well-being as they engage in the sticky details of skillbuilding. *Boys and girls, isn't this exciting! Just look at the big pile of books you already can read.*

The longer and more complex a child's reading assignments become, the more he needs a collection of short, beautifully structured books that appeal to his imagination, his esthetic yearnings, and his reading prowess. The *InstantReaders* offer three levels of books to satisfy these needs. *The levels must not be confused with grade levels.*

The levels with their ordinal designations simply suggest the comparative complexity of language patterns and symbolisms. Lucky is the child who has available all three levels so that he can wander back and forth at will, finding out about his tastes in art and language, his needs for books that he can read in a few minutes, his yen for humor to leaven the more serious parts of his day, his joy in quick success: *I can do it! I can do it! I can do it!* In the midst of struggling with fractions or remedial reading, for example, a child can restore his belief in himself by picking up a book that has pretensions to linguistic excellence and still can be mastered *inside and out.*

a child has continuing need

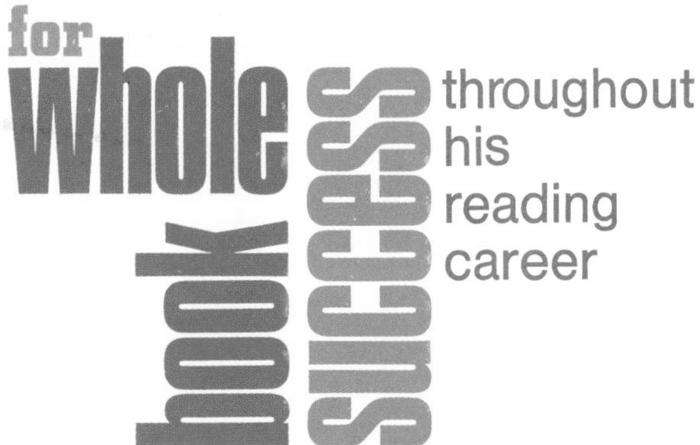

an emerging reader needs a battery of books that he can zoom through with joyous familiarity

Every child, particularly in the early reaches of reading instruction, needs a battery of books that he can "read on his own" for personal pleasure. Too many times children spend an entire semester learning to read a single book, then even before they have had the pleasure of returning to it time and again, "just for fun," they are hurried on to the next reader. As important as choosing books from the library can be, this does not take the place in the young reader's life of having constantly available a corps of favorite books that can be read without any awareness of word/unlocking problems. Taste is not formed by being hurried from book to book, but rather by knowing which book you want to return to again and again, and by knowing which sentences, which pictures, which words you like better than others. Those of us who seriously care about helping children learn to read might question what we accomplish by teaching the so-called reading skills if we "turn out" children who don't of their own volition reach/out for books. Joyous familiarity with a corps of select books is probably the greatest motivation factor in nurturing a developing reader.

Young readers need the thrust of literary fellowship

The literary fellowship engendered by continuous exposure to a collection of books that are being read and enjoyed and discussed in a variety of circumstances and settings is the milieu in which sensitive and mature readers thrive. Imagine the delight of a child who cocks an ear and hears two friends reading aloud *Whistle, Mary, Whistle*, an old favorite of his. Or imagine the glow of awareness children have when a teacher paraphrases Old Mother Middle Muddle, "*Now ... let's see ... what were we going to do? ... O, yes ... now I remember ... we were going to go home.*"

Consider, in contrast, the divisive competitive overtones in a classroom where certain books belong only to the "high" reading group, others to the "low." And consider the unhealthy emotional atmosphere when two good friends can't share the same books because they are divided by reading groups or reading levels. The *InstantReaders* cut across such levels and belong to all children in a classroom. Not that *every* child must read *every* book, but that his reading career needs the stretch and comfort and human enjoyment of a commonly/shared corps of literature.

DRAMATIC CUMULATIVE REPETITIONS REPETITIONS REPETITIONS REPETITIONS OF LANGUAGE

help children anticipate (and thereby decode) the printed page

Most of the *InstantReaders* have obvious repetitive struc-tures

which immediately propel children into anticipating the next line or the next
rhyming word or the next episode. Naturally this is not an infallible method of
decoding print, but it is one impressive experience in helping children know that they
can trust print because of its underlying structures.

In a dark dark woods there is a dark dark house,
In the dark dark house there is a dark dark stair,
Down the dark dark stair ...

Even on first acquaintance, a child will predict that
1) the pattern of this phrasing will maintain throughout the story,
2) that all of the objects will be described as *dark dark*,
3) that the last part of each line becomes the first part of the next line.

Imagine the child's surprise, therefore, to discover that the *spirit* in the
dark dark bottle is not *dark dark*, but is *evil*. Couched as this var-
iation is within so many dependable repetitions, it does not
cause a child to lose faith in his method of predicting
language, but rather suggests to him that there are
also other methods of decoding language that
will be helpful. His curiosity, therefore,
is piqued to find multiple ways of
unlocking print. *Children, isn't*
it interesting that the au-
thor didn't call the
spirit dark dark.
How can you tell by looking at the print that he did not say dark dark?

language skills are best learned in the shape and swing of a sentence

Children intuitively know that language is best learned in the shape and swing of sentences. This is how they learned to talk. Most five-year-olds already own a wide range of sentence structures. If, however, a child doesn't have a sufficient repertoire of oral language structures, the school's first job is to enter them into his ear in such enticing ways that he will reach out to claim them as his own. The sentence patterns in the *InstantReaders*, *sharply* focused by predictable story structure, range from the simplest noun-verb construction, I *sing*, to the highly complex pattern, "*O joy!*" *said the fox*, "*when the rooster comes out to swallow the bee, I'll grab him by the neck.*" Complicated though this latter sentence may seem, couched as it is within the dependable structure of the book, it is more easily available to children than oversimplified sentences that are not couched in dependable story structure.

dependable
schemes of
rhyme
and
rhythm
help children
read words they
didn't know they knew

Just as children intake oral language more easily when it is in rhyme-y or jingle-y form, so they find themselves more at ease with storybooks of similar design. Having perceived that a story rhymes in couplets or in alternate lines, children are strongly prepared to speak and to read the rhyming words throughout the story, even before they can handle the rest of the phrasing: *I dance. I sing.*
I run. I wing.
I skip. I jump.
I hop. I hump.
This type of rhyme scheme is a child's most reliable clue for handling the dance of words in this story. The word *hump*, for example, falls easily into place in spite of its unusualness. The rhyme and rhythm pattern dictates that the word must be a one-syllable word rhyming with *jump*. As the child goes further into reading and learns about beginning consonants, short vowel sounds, and the usefulness of configuration and picture clues, he will bring any or all of these into play as he unlocks an unknown rhyming word, but it nonetheless is the rhyming clue that undergirds his whole decoding process.

The recognition of a rhyming word within literary structure is qualitatively different from studying isolated lists of rhyming words. Literary structure gives the word a linguistic mooring and integrity that it can never achieve in isolation. Interestingly enough, an experience of this kind may subsequently trigger children into making lists of rhyming words, but this activity is permeated with the awareness that isolated words are dead things and need the thrust of linguistic structure to claim their being. It is this kind of knowledge gleaned from *InstantReader* experiences that contributes significantly to a child's emerging generalizations about language and how it works.

emerging readers find quick success with stories that are

Simply by living in our culture, children have certain built-in structures going for them that can be translated to advantage in learning to read. They know, for example, that the hours of the day, the days of the week, the months and seasons of the year, the number system, and the alphabet have dependable sequences. Sooner or later the children become familiar with and use these sequences like another hand or foot or eye or ear in dealing with the outside world. The *InstantReader* program exploits certain of these structures as another way to help children appreciate the fact that the recognition of underlying structure

patterned on familiar cultural sequences

is an aid in decoding print. *Sunday, Sunday, I like Sunday, Sunday the first day of the week. Monday, Monday, I Like Monday, Monday the second day of the week. . . .* From this point in the story, a child needs only his knowledge of ordinal numbers to 7, and the names and sequence of the days of the week to read seven spreads of print. The intrigue of the last half of the book, *Monday, Monday* in which these familiar structures are reversed and in other ways played upon, highlights in intriguing ways the usefulness of familiar structures in unlocking unfamiliar new print.

remedial reading should begin with every child role-playing himself as a

At whatever time a child is assigned to remedial reading, he needs immediately to know that he can read an entire book. Chances are that he has plodded through month after month of reading instruction, never having the feeling of wholebook*success*. The *Instant-Readers* provide the opportunity for a sharp turnabout in that detrimental course of action. A child can, in fact, read an entire book on the very first day. Luckily there is nothing "firstgradish" or "scaled vocabulary-ish" about the *Instant Readers.* Many fifth graders who are offended, for example, by scaled down stories about fake cowboys will pit all of their intuitions toward figuring out the author's scheme of putting *Silly Goose and the Holidays* together, sensing

successful reader of books

that the author was interested in a literary outcome and not an easy-vocabulary manipulation. The integrity of the literary structure of *Silly Goose* comes through at whatever age the reader. Moreover, the *InstantReaders* free a child from the grip of having only a single word-unlocking skill (sounding out the word) and help him add a wide ranging repertoire of structural decoding skills to what he already possesses. *Boys and girls, this may look like an easy book to you, but we're going to do fifthgrade things with it. How long has it been since you figured out the scheme an author had in mind when he put his book together? Figuring out the scheme of a story may be one of your most useful reading skills.* You will be surprised at how fast a child grasps the awareness that he can read.

when a book involves a child  Esthetically its message has more meaning.

Esthetic involvement touches you "where you live." It defies convention and logic and academic know-how, yet it has everything to do with learning because it wells out of a person's strivings for human kinship. The ingenuous, cumulative coupling of sequences in *Brown Bear, Brown Bear,* is an example:

Brown bear, brown bear, what do you see?
I see a redbird looking at me.
Redbird, redbird, what do you see?
I see a yellow duck looking at me.
Yellow duck, yellow duck, what do you see?
I see a blue horse looking at me, etc.

The coupling has nothing and yet everything to do with reading. Momentarily banished are the restrictions of print, the preoccupation with eye movements from left to right, and "today's new words" drill. The literature creates its own life. The linguistic dance of the question and answer in *Brown Bear* is so pervasive and appealing that the reader is caught up in it and responds without labored awareness of technicalities and rules. And consider the delight and *pulling-power* of *Tricks or Treats?* which playfully rewrites jelly beans as *belly jeans*, lollipops as *pollilops*, popcorn balls as *copborn palls*, all in intriguing sweeps of language which twist and curlicue and bend back upon themselves as part of the pictorial design. The important meanings of these and other *InstantReaders* are not the story facts. It is irrelevant which animal Brown Bear saw or what trick was performed on which floor of the apartment house. The humanly worthwhile meanings are found in the playfulness of the language, in the interrelations of color and design and story evolvements, and in the inculcated awareness that life is worth living.

And Now for the very FIRST TIME • YOU CAN GET *Bill Martin* RECORDINGS •

"Read-along" cassettes and L.P. recordings, adding insightful and memorable linguistic dimensions to each of the *Instant Readers,* are now available. These are the first recordings that Bill Martin, America's distinguished storyteller and creator of provocative oral-aural reading materials, has made for classroom use. As you can imagine from knowing Bill Martin's *Owl Books, Sounds of Language Reader's,* and now the *Instant Readers,* his "read-along" recordings involve children esthetically, linguistically and humanly in the miracle of man's greatest invention—language. Your children will be reading along with Bill Martin, responding to and inculcating his love of language—all the while learning how to read with accuracy, joy and security. As their eyes see what their ears hear and their tongues speak, children will deposit into their linguistic storehouses, model sentence and story patterns that evoke pervasive skill development in all of the language arts—reading, writing, speaking, and listening.

INSTANT READERS

LEVEL 2 Teacher's Guide

Discussion of each book

PART 2

Whistle Mary, Whistle

adapted by Bill Martin Jr. with pictures by Emanuele Luzzati and handlettering by Ray Barber

"Whistle, Mary, whistle,
and you shall have a cow."
"I can't whistle, Mother,
because I don't know how."

"Whistle, Mary, whistle,
and you shall have a pig."
"I can't whistle, Mother,
because I'm not so big."

"Whistle, Mary, whistle,
and you shall have a sheep."
"I can't whistle, Mother,
because I am asleep."

"Whistle, Mary, whistle,
and you shall have a trout."
"I can't whistle, Mother,
because my tooth is out."

"Whistle, Mary, whistle,
and you shall have a rabbit."
"I can't whistle, Mother,
because I've lost the habit."

"Whistle, Mary, whistle,
and you shall have a goat."
"I can't whistle, Mother,
because it hurts my throat."

"Whistle, Mary, whistle,
and you shall have a daisy."
"I can't whistle, Mother,
because it looks so crazy."

"Whistle, Mary, whistle,
and you shall have a pickle."
"I can't whistle, Mother,
because it makes me tickle."

"Whistle, Mary, whistle,
and you shall have some honey."
"I can't whistle, Mother,
because it feels so funny."

"Whistle, Mary, whistle,
and you shall have some bread."
"I can't whistle, Mother,
because I'm standing on my head."

"Whistle, Mary, whistle,
and you shall have a pie."
"I can't whistle, Mother,
because my mouth is dry."

"Whistle, Mary, whistle,
and you shall have some gold."
"I can't whistle, Mother,
because I'm not that old."

"Whistle, Mary, whistle,
and you shall have the moon."
"I can't whistle, Mother,
because I've lost the tune."

"Whistle, Mary, whistle,
and you shall have a man."
"Tweet, tweet, tweet, tweet, tweet,
I just found out I can."

The rhyme scheme and repetition in *Whistle, Mary, Whistle* are so dependable that the children will probably be chiming in with you long before you finish the first reading.

1. **Reading joyfully from cover to cover,** p. 76. *Let's read it again* is a likely response to the children's first reading of the book. These follow-up readings can easily turn into choral reading with some children reading Mother's part, others reading Mary's part. The children may be interested in portraying character traits in both Mary and Mother as they read their lines. Don't be surprised if their reading leads to skipping, dancing and singing. These are all highly successful ways for depositing language patterns into the bloodstream.

2. **Innovating on literary structure,** p. 77. If the children do not spontaneously suggest innovations, certain open-ended remarks will help them get started.

   Supposing Mother didn't want Mary to whistle. What else could she ask her to do?

   Supposing it wasn't Mother and Mary talking. Who else might it be?

   What else might be offered as rewards?

3. **Analyzing literary structure,** p. 79. Because it is so obvious, the children will probably have little difficulty verbalizing their recognition of the underlying structure of this book.

4. **Analyzing rhythmical structure,** p. 85. Along with a

rhyme scheme, this book has a dependable rhythmical structure which helps to predict vocabulary. Mary's responses to her mother, for example, follow the beat of her first response:

because I don't know how *because I'm not so big*

Many children develop their sensitivity to language rhythm as one of their ways for attacking unknown words.

5. **Analyzing sentence structure,** p. 86. Here are two classic sentence models for the children to transform. Simply write Mother's command or Mary's response on the board and invite the children to substitute naming words for naming words, action words for action words, etc. Even the connecting word *because* can invite interesting substitutions such as *since*, *or*, etc. Won't it be interesting to discover how the meaning of a sentence can alter by changing only the connecting word?

6. **Analyzing word structure,** p. 90. You may wish to begin a list of words ending in *le* which are found in the Level II *Instant Readers: whistle, little, castle, Middle Muddle, etc.*

8. **Responding to art,** p. 94. Children who have read Level I *Instant Readers* may recognize Emanuele Luzzati as the same artist who illustrated *When It Rains, It Rains*. Whether this is their first or second encounter with Luzzati, they will probably enjoy discussing details in his childlike crayon drawings. He seems so free and unworried about details like staying inside the black line. How nice if children have this freedom!

A Spooky Story

by Bill Martin Jr. with pictures by Albert John Pucci and handlettering by Ray Barber

Out of the shadows, out of the flum
comes one creeping cat.

Out of the shadows, out of the flum
come two sweeping bats.

Out of the shadows, out of the flum
come three moaning ghosts.

Out of the shadows, out of the flum
come four groaning goblins.

Out of the shadows, out of the flum
come five screaming vampires.

Out of the shadows, out of the flum
come six screeching owls.

Out of the shadows, out of the flum
come seven shrieking witches.

Out of the shadows, out of the flum
come eight floating skeletons.

Out of the shadows, out of the flum
come nine howling werewolves.

Out of the shadows, out of the flum
come ten evil spirits.

Turning about, burning about,
flimming about, flumming about.
Screaming about, sleaming about,
wailing about, kwailing about.
Howling,
yowling,
cowling,
prowling.

Then back into the flum they come.

A Spooky Story is hung together with repetition, cardinal number and spooky vocabulary. Albert John Pucci's spooky paintings are so much a part of the story it seems impossible to separate them from the words. As you read aloud to the children, let your voice take on the same exciting spookiness that permeates this story. After reading aloud, the book is available for wide-ranging follow-up activities, some of which are suggested here.

1. **Reading joyfully from cover to cover,** p. 76. Reading from cover to cover means more when there is an element of drama in the reading. Story and sentence and word patterns become more firmly entrenched in the children's linguistic repertoires and are therefore more available for later analysis activities. *A Spooky Story* certainly lends itself to dramatic reading. Invite the children to elongate the vowels, invent sound effects and in other ways capitalize on the language and mood of the story. You will have to be the judge of how much spookiness the children can tolerate. Better save their spooky reading for a rainy day that needs brightening if the children seem to have had enough spookiness for one day. There is a happy balance between denying children the excitement of scary emotions in an effort to protect them and surrounding them with more of these emotions than they can handle. Your good judgment and your willingness to pick up clues from the children will help you achieve this balance.

2. **Innovating on literary structure,** p. 77. In no time at all, children can be dictating or writing their own versions of *A Spooky Story*. As a matter of fact

> *Out of the ocean, out of the waves comes one lovable mermaid*

may be the quickest way to momentarily dispel the spooky atmosphere if this seems desirable.

3. **Analyzing literary structure,** p. 79. Children can easily discuss the author's plan for putting this book together. Triggering questions might be:

> *Children, when did you first hunch that certain language was going to be repeated in this story?*
>
> *When did you discover how the author was using numbers in his story?*

There are no right answers to these questions. Each child needs to be free to tell who he is as an analyzer of literary structure.

5. **Analyzing sentence structure,** p. 86. Transforming the basic sentence in this book will help children appreciate sentences with introductory phrases as well as the position and function of describing words.

Out of the shadows, out of the flum come two creeping cats.
Into the water into the pool jump six shivering boys.

6. **Analyzing word structure,** p. 90. What fun you and the children will have figuring out how Bill Martin determined the spelling of his make-up words! Invite them to find words in the English language which would suggest the two *m's* in *flimming* and *flumming,* the *ow* in *cowling,* the *ai* in *kwailing,* etc.

7. **Responding to typographical intrigue,** p. 92. As the type floats in and out and around with the spooky creatures, the children learn in impressive ways that those squiggles which appear on the pages of a book are an important part of the meaning. What a nice time for the children to experiment with their own floating sentences or spooky writing.

8. **Responding to art,** p. 94. Children will enjoy picture-reading this book, making appropriate spooky noises and conversation as they go. They may enjoy discussing the artist's various ways for communicating the mood he wants and they may want to try their own hands at mood pictures.

City Song

by James Steel Smith illustrated by Fuka Hervert

many windows
  many floors
many people
  many doors
many vendors
  many streets
many flavors
  many treats
many taxis
  many buses
many prices
  many fusses
many outings
  many walkings
many sittings
  many talkings

many noises
    many bangings
many whistles
    many clangings
many workers
    families many . . .

. . . trucks . . . airplanes . . . trains . . . bridges . . . tunnels
. . . schools . . . churches . . . children . . . babies . . . parks
. . . dogs . . . cats . . . stoplights . . . friendships . . .

many of everything

manymanymanymanymanymanymanymanymanymanymanymany
manymanymanymanymanymanymanymanymanymanymanymany
manymanymanymanymanymanymanymanymanymanymanymany

many of any

City Song is a book that organizes around a language pattern (*many* of this thing and *many* of that thing) and a rhyme scheme. The language is not necessarily the kind that will deposit itself in the children's linguistic storehouses on a first reading, especially if they are pondering Fuka Hervert's intriguing city art at the same time. You may wish to read the book several times before inviting the children into any or all of the follow-up activities.

1. **Reading joyfully from cover to cover,** p. 76. At some point the children will enjoy reading this book from cover to cover with linguistic abandon. They may assign solo parts for choral reading and at other times read it as a total group, using dramatic intonations and voice levels to produce the insistent feeling of *many*.

2. **Innovating on literary structure,** p. 77. This structure lends itself to as many innovations as there are children in your class. A change of the word *many* to *angry*, for example, has a whole new story going. On the other hand, it may be the A B C B rhyme scheme which the children decide to borrow as they create stories and poems which do not in any other way resemble *City Song*.

3. **Analyzing literary structure,** p. 79. Because the rhyme scheme is so easily seen in this poem

many windows	A	*many people*	C
many floors	B	*many doors*	B

the children may enjoy labelling the lines as indicated above, and begin a discussion and understanding of this way for ana-

lyzing rhyme scheme. Don't press for exact and total understanding of this relatively abstract concept. Look on your discussion as a beginning of many explorations into the intrigue and excitement of rhyme schemes.

5. **Analyzing sentence structure,** p. 86. You can help children come to a useful appreciation of sentence structure by inviting them to make sentences out of the phrases found on these pages.

6. **Analyzing word structure,** p. 90. The words *many* and *any* provide useful opportunities for discussing the intriguing fact that the English language isn't always as regular as we'd like to believe it is.

> *Children, is it any wonder boys and girls have problems with spelling and pronouncing words in a language that can be as cuckoo as ours!*

This may be the beginning of a bulletin board list of other "cuckoo" words which are best learned as sight vocabulary and not by rules for "sounding them out."

8. **Responding to art,** p. 94. This book deserves several picture-readings. Each time the children pore over Fuka Hervert's delightful city scenes, they will find new happenings to discuss. Unlike city pictures which simply show buildings and people and transportation as objects, the Hervert pictures create relationships. Your room may come alive with reading charts of the children's dictation in response to the triggering question: *what is happening in this picture?*

Old Mother Middle-Muddle

by Bill Martin Jr. with pictures by Don Madden

Old Mother Middle Muddle put down her knitting
and went to the kitchen to brew a cup of tea.

"O joy!" said the mouse,
"when Old Mother Middle Muddle makes a cup of tea,
she's sure to have a cookie and drop some crumbs for me."

"O joy!" said the cat,
"when the mouse comes out to eat the crumbs,
I'll pounce on him!"

"O joy!" said the dog,
"when the cat comes out to pounce on the mouse,
I'll bite her."

"O joy!" said the pig,
"when the dog comes out to bite the cat,
I'll poke him in the side."

"O joy!" said the cow,
"when the pig comes out to poke the dog,
I'll hook him with my horns."

"O joy!" said the donkey,
"when the cow comes out to hook the dog,
I'll kick her over the fence."

"O joy!" said the bee,
"when the donkey comes out to kick the cow,
I'll sting him on the nose."

"O joy!" said the rooster,
"when the bee comes out to sting the donkey,
I'll swallow him for dinner."

"O joy!" said the fox,
"when the rooster comes out to swallow the bee,
I'll grab him by the neck."

"O joy!" said the goose,
"when the fox comes out to grab the rooster,
I'll beat him with my wings."

"O joy!" said the goat,
"when the goose comes out to beat the fox,
I'll butt him over my head."

"O joy!" said the turkey,
"when the goat comes out to butt the goose,
I'll peck him on the chin."

Old Mother Middle Muddle, walked into the kitchen,
"Now . . . let's see . . . what was I going to do?
. . . O yes . . . now I remember . . . wash my sox."

Old Mother Middle Muddle is built on an interlocking pattern. Like *Silly Goose and the Holidays* in the Level I *Instant Readers*, each new episode creates a dependable relationship with the episode that went before. Once the children are aware of this pattern, their eyes and ears are open to discover what action the new animal will take against the animal in the preceding episode.

1. **Reading joyfully from cover to cover,** p. 76. Even though the children catch on to the basic pattern of this story, they may need two or three readings before they have the specific language for each animal's action. Encourage them to read along with you, intoning the announcement of each new animal as they see fit. Once they have devised choral reading assignments for each character, won't it be fun to help them use voice and gesture to portray the characteristics of each animal and Old Mother Middle Muddle!

2. **Innovating on literary structure,** p. 77 and
3. **Analyzing literary structure,** p. 79. Analyzing the interlocking relationship between the episodes in this story may come before the children embark on their own innovations. However, you may have children who will intuitively sense the structure and create a similar story without verbalizing their understanding of how it works. You may wish to borrow *Brown Bear, Brown Bear, What Do You See?* or *Silly Goose and the Holidays* from the Level I *Instant Readers* to launch a full-fledged discussion of this form of literary structure and of the help a person has in word-unlocking once he recognizes the structure.

5. **Analyzing sentence structure,** p. 86

"Oh joy," said the rooster.
Mercy me *(My goodness)*
Oh boy *(Good grief)*

Here is a worthwhile sentence to put on the bulletin board, inviting the children to transform the sentence by substituting introductory ejaculations. It is entirely possible that your list will grow to be as long as your bulletin board.

6. **Analyzing word structure,** p. 90. If the children began lists of words ending in *le* when they read *Whistle, Mary, Whistle,* now is a good time to become more analytical about these *le* words. Isn't it interesting, for example, that all of the consonants are sounded in *little, Middle, Muddle,* while they aren't in *castle* and *whistle.* This may begin a search for other words ending in *le (puddle, muddle, whistle, thistle)* with observations about the construction and pronunciations of the words.

8. **Responding to art,** p. 94. The children may be interested to know that Don Madden did not want a sharp black line to outline the objects in his pictures. He purposely prepared his art so that the lines would be soft and almost shaggy. What effect do the children think this has on the illustrations? Do some of them prefer sharp lines? These kinds of observations and choice-making sessions help children know what they do and don't prefer in drawings and paintings—a necessary step in developing esthetic awareness and taste.

The Longest Journey in the World

by William Barrett Morris with pictures by Betty Fraser and handlettering by Ray Barber

One morning as the sun was coming up,
a little caterpillar said to himself,
"I am going on a long journey."
He crawled and he crawled and he crawled.
He crawled over a high mountain.
He crawled into a deep valley.
He crawled around a huge castle.
He crawled up a high wall.
He crawled across a wide river.
He crawled under an iron fence.
He crawled over a fallen tree.
He crawled past a sleeping dragon.
He crawled through a dense forest.
He crawled and he crawled and he crawled.
That night as the sun was going down,
the little caterpillar wondered how far he had come.
So he climbed a tall Chinaberry tree to look back.
"I am truly amazed," he said to himself.
"This is the longest journey in the world."

The Longest Journey in The World creates an intriguing relationship between art and text, and even between reality and perceived reality. The children will probably have many reminiscences of times when their view of a situation seemed more real than the situation itself.

1. **Reading joyfully from cover to cover,** p. 76. The basic sentence pattern in this book is so dependable that children will have no problem reading along with you once they have heard the story. Invite them to experiment with various ways for intoning the describing word in each line:

   He climbed over a *high* mountain.

   This will add both to the excitement of the reading and to the children's appreciation of describing words in sentences.

2. **Innovating on literary structure,** p. 77. The children can undoubtedly spin stories about their own "long" journeys—their first trip around the block, their first train or plane ride. Some might become involved in imaginative excursions, borrowing the author's notion of choosing a creature as a main character. The children will undoubtedly vary in their ways for patterning the story—some borrowing the author's notion of a single sentence for each episode, others choosing as many sentences as they need to satisfactorily tell the story as they want it told.

5. **Analyzing sentence structure,** p. 86. The basic sentence in this story is well worth transforming and analyzing. Each word performs a clear function in the sentence. As the children substitute action words, naming words, describing words and connecting words you will have a fine opportunity to help them verbalize their understanding of what the various words do. The word *over*, for example, connects *He climbed* with *a high mountain*. Now might be a profitable time for the children to sort out their word cards, sorting them into naming words, action words, describing words and connecting words. They can then examine each category to see if they need to add words from *The Longest Journey in the World* or from their sentence transformations.

7. **Responding to typographical intrigue,** p. 92. The gentle curving of the type adds visual dimensions to the movement of the caterpillar. Perhaps the children would like to experiment with arrangements of type that portray movement.

8. **Responding to art,** p. 94. The sheer beauty of Betty Fraser's drawings gives a person the feeling that he too has journeyed in the little caterpillar's backyard loveliness. The children's appreciation of the illustrations may well be expressed more in *oohs* and *ahs* than in analytical discussion. What a nice way for them to show that the esthetic dimensions have truly entered their bloodstreams.

Isn't it interesting how the artist's paintings of exact objects help give meaning to this book. What do you suppose would have happened to the meaning if the hose couldn't be identified as a hose, the flower pot as a flower pot, etc.?

King of the Mountain

by Bill Martin Jr. with pictures by Ivor Parry

It began to rain.

A boy looked out of the window and said,
"I'm the king of the puddle."

A frog looked out of the puddle and said,
"I'm the king of the pond."

A minnow looked out of the pond and said,
"I'm the king of the lake."

A turtle looked out of the lake and said,
"I'm the king of the river."

A crocodile looked out of the river and said,
"I'm the king of the ocean."

A whale looked out of the ocean and said,
"I'm the king of the mountain."

A dragon looked down from the mountain and said,
"I'm the king of the hilltops."

A leopard looked down from the hilltops and said,
"I'm the king of the desert."

A camel looked over the desert and said,
"I'm the king of the grasslands."

A lion looked out from the grasslands and said,
"I'm the king of the jungle."

An elephant looked out of the jungle and said,
"I'm the king of the world."

An astronaut looked down on the world and said,
"I'm the king of the universe."

A star looked down on the astronaut and said,
"What on earth are they talking about?"

King of the Mountain is hung together with repetition and a series of interlocking episodes. In no time the children will be reading along with you, using both the art and the literary structure to give them clues. Encourage them to portray the personalities of the various characters as they read their boasts, including the assignment of solo parts for choral reading.

2. 3. **Innovating on literary structure,** p. 77 and **Analyzing literary structure,** p. 79. Some children may be triggered by the "King of the Mountain" idea and write or tell their own "King" stories with or without paying any attention to the way the episodes interlock with one another in the original book. Other children may be intrigued with the underlying structure, and after discussing their understanding of how it works, may wish to create other "interlocking" stories. You may wish to remind them again of what they discovered about the interlocking structure of *Old Mother Middle Muddle* and the children may have other interlocking stories to add to the discussion.

5. **Analyzing sentence structure,** p. 86.

I'm	*the*	*king*	*of*	*the*	*mountain.*
He's		*husband*			*queen.*
You're		*snake*	*in*		*grass.*

As the children transform this sentence, they can learn much about the various forms of pronouns, about agreement between pronoun and verb, about singular and plural forms, etc.

And best of all, they intake these learnings as they are actively experimenting with sentences rather than trying to memorize rules.

6. **Analyzing word structure,** p. 90. Now is a good time for the children to add interesting geography words to their word card collections: *mountain. grasslands. ocean.* Invite them to make their own observations about each of these words, deciding how best to remember their printed form or spelling pattern.

7. **Responding to typographical intrigue,** p. 92. While most of the type in *King of the Mountain* lies in conventional placement on the page, the beauty and intrigue in the intertwining of type and art on the last page of the story can invite exciting experimentation from the children. After inviting their response to this page, you may wish to go back to the title page where Bill Martin also followed the shape of the star in placing type on the page.

8. **Responding to art,** p. 94. How the children will enjoy Ivor Parry's pictures! The smug look on the boy. The position of the crocodile. The fierceness of the dragon. They may wish to create their own lions looking out of grasslands or their own astronauts floating through space. Don't be surprised if it takes them considerable time to manage movement and position and space the way the artist does. And don't be surprised at their pleasure in trying again and again to create the effects they want.

Old Devil Wind

by Bill Martin Jr. paintings by Robert J. Lee
lettering by Ray Barber

One dark and stormy night
Ghost floated out of the wall
and he began to WAIL.

Stool said,
"Ghost, Ghost, why do you wail?"
Ghost said,
"It's a dark and stormy night
and so I wail."
And Stool said,
"Then I shall thump."
So Stool began to THUMP!

Broom said,
"Stool, why do you thump?"
Stool said,
"It is a dark and stormy night
and Ghost wails
and so I thump."
Broom said,
"Then I shall swish."
So Broom began to SWISH.

Candle said,
"Broom, why do you swish?"
Broom said,
"It is a dark and stormy night
and Ghost wails
and Stool thumps
and so I swish."
Candle said,
"Then I shall flicker."
And Candle began to flicker.

Fire said,
"Candle, why do you flicker?"
Candle said,
"It is a dark and stormy night
and Ghost wails
and Stool thumps
and Broom swishes
and so I flicker."
Fire said,
"Then I shall smoke."
and Fire began to SMOKE.

Window said,
"Fire, why do you smoke?"
Fire said,
"It is a dark and stormy night
and Ghost wails
and Stool thumps
and Broom swishes
and Candle flickers
and so I smoke."
Window said,
"Then I shall rattle."
And Window began to RATTLE.

Floor said,
"Window, why do you rattle?"
Window said,
"It is a dark and stormy night
and Ghost wails
and Stool thumps
and Broom swishes
and Candle flickers
and Fire smokes
and so I rattle."
Floor said,
"Then I shall creak."
And Floor began to CREAK.

Door said,
"Floor, why do you creak?"
Floor said,
"It is a dark and stormy night
and Ghost wails
and Stool thumps
and Broom swishes
and Candle flickers
and Fire smokes
and Window rattles
and so I creak."
Door said,
"Then I shall slam."
And Door began to SLAMMM.

Owl said,
"Door, why do you slam?"
Door said,
"It is a dark and stormy night
and Ghost wails
and Stool thumps
and Broom swishes
and Candle flickers
and Fire Smokes
and Window rattles
and Floor creaks
and so I slam."
Owl said,
"Then I shall hoot."
And Owl began to HOOOOOT.

Witch said,
"Owl, why do you hoot?"
Owl said,
"It is a dark and stormy night
and Ghost wails
and Stool thumps
and Broom swishes
and Candle flickers
and Fire smokes
and Window rattles
and Floor creaks
and Door slams
and so I hoot."
Witch said,
"THEN I SHALL FLY
AROUND THE HOUSE."

(continued)

(continued)

Wind said,
"Witch, why do you fly around the house?"
Witch said,
"It is a dark and stormy night
and Ghost wails
and Stool thumps
and Broom swishes
and Candle flickers
and Fire smokes
and Window rattles
and Floor creaks
and Door slams
and Owl hoots
and so I fly around the house."
Wind said,
"Then I shall blow."
And Wind began to BLOW
AND HE BLEW AWAY THE GHOST
AND THE HOUSE
AND THE BROOOOOMMMMMMM
AND THE STOOOOOOOOLLLLLLL
AND THE CANDLEEEEEEEEEEE
AND THE FIREEEEEEEEEEEE
AND THE WINDOWWWWWWWW
AND THE FLOOOOORRRRRRRR
AND THE DOOOOOORRRRRRRR
AND THE OOOOOWWWLLLLLLL
AND THE WITCHHHHHHH
AND THEY DIDN'T COME BACK
'TIL HHHHHHHHHHH HHHHALLOWWEEN NIGHTTTTT.

Old Devil Wind is organized around a dependable cumulative structure. Each new episode repeats everything that appeared in preceding episodes before adding the new thought. The children will probably recognize the pattern long before you finish your first reading aloud of the book and they will be chiming in with you. Then comes the fun of the follow-up activities.

1. **Reading joyfully from cover to cover,** p. 76. Actually, this is a book to read *spookily* from cover to cover. Invite the children to use all of their ingenuity to suggest the *wail* of the ghost, the *thump* of the stool, the *swish* of the broom, etc. Before long they will be suggesting choral reading arrangements with different children taking turns at giving solo interpretations of the various conversations. They may become interested in making a puppet show of *Old Devil Wind*, using all of their imagination in creating the characters, the movement, and the sound effects. The more reasons children find for reading a book over and over with dramatic overtones, the more firmly the language patterns become available for their own speaking and writing as well as for analytical activities.

2. **Innovating on literary structure,** p. 77. The intrigue of the literary structure can prompt the children to try their hands at cumulative writing. If you feel that reading other cumulative stories would be helpful before the children embark on their own adventures, you might read *The House that Jack Built (Sounds Around the Clock)* or *The Old Woman and Her Pig (Sounds of Laughter)*.

3. **Analyzing literary structure,** p. 79. Encourage the children to use their own language in discussing how the author put his story together. You may wish to start a reading-table collection or bulletin board list of other stories and books built on this same structure.

5. **Analyzing sentence structure,** p. 86.

Ghost	*came*	*out*	*of*	*the*	*wall*	*and*	*he*	*began*	*to*	*wail.*
Henry	*jumped*	*into*			*pond*					*swim.*
	ran	*around*			*block*					*puff.*

This is a useful sentence pattern for helping children see how connecting words (*out of*, *into*, *around*) tie words together.

jumped into the pond
ran around the block.

It is this kind of recognition of how words work together in patterns that helps children develop skill in reading and writing the English language.

6. **Analyzing word structure,** p. 90 and **Responding to**
7. **typographical intrigue,** p. 92. The typographical intrigue in this book invites all sorts of excursions into the structure of words. The extra o's in *brooooooom* and *stoooool* impressively suggest the importance of medial vowels in words. The extra *m*'s and *l*'s at the end offer the same opportunity for discussing endings. The hand-lettered action words (*wail, thump, swish* etc.) exaggerate the important notion that words have shapes.

When word analysis has the extra dimension of esthetic intrigue, important learnings are more lasting.

8. **Responding to art,** p. 94. The children may enjoy knowing that the artist painted his pictures twice the size of the pages in the book in order to get the effects he wanted. This may invite experimentation with large and small paintings as well as with creating mood pictures. If the illustrations trigger a lot of free-flowing conversation about the various fears children encounter, encourage the children to say what they will. They may wish to create illustrations to go with their personal fears. This kind of getting one's fears out in the open is one way of making them more manageable.

The Little Disaster

An old jingle with pictures by John Rombola
and handlettering by Ray Barber

Once there lived a little man,
Where a little river ran,
And he had a little farm and little dairy O!

And he had a little plough,
And a little dappled cow,
Which he often called his pretty little Fairy O!

And his dog he called Fidelle,
For he loved his master well.
And he had a little pony for his pleasure O!

In a sty not very big
He'd a frisky little pig,
Which he often called his little piggy treasure O!

Once his little maiden, Ann,
With her pretty little can,
Went a-milking when the morning sun was beaming O!

When she fell, I know not how,
But she tumbled o'er the plough,
And the cow was quite astonished at her screaming O!

Little maid cried out in vain
While the milk ran o'er the plain,
Little pig ran grunting after it so gaily O!

While the little dog behind
For a share was much inclined,
So he pulled back squealing piggy by the taily O!

Such a clatter now began
As alarmed the little man,
Who came capering from out his little stable O!

Pony trod on doggy's toes,
Doggy snapped at piggy's nose,
Piggy made as great a noise as he was able O!

Then, to make the story short,
Little pony with a snort
Lifted up his little heels so very clever O!

And the man he tumbled down,
And he nearly cracked his crown,
And this only made the matter worse than ever O!

The Little Disaster is hung together with a lilting rhythm, a rhyme scheme and a story line. The children may enjoy discussing the fact that here is a story that doesn't "turn out right" in the end, like so many stories do. How could a story called *The Little Disaster* end in anything but a disaster!

1. **Reading joyfully from cover to cover,** p. 76. Some children may remember this story as a song and may burst into singing as you read. How nice! If the children have not heard the story before, it may take a few readings before they can manage to read independently from cover to cover.

2. 3. 4. 5. **Innovating on literary structure,** p. 77, **Analyzing literary structure,** p. 79, **Analyzing rhythmical structure,** p. 85 and **Analyzing sentence structure,** p. 86. As the children experiment with innovations on *The Little Disaster*, they will undoubtedly be discussing the rhyme scheme and experimenting with the rhythmical and sentence structure. Reading the story in duh-duh fashion, for example:

Duh duh duh-duh-duh-duh-duh
Once there lived-a-lit-tle-man

will give them a feeling of the underlying beat, and they may wish to try putting new words to it. On the other hand, they may begin by transforming the opening sentence. Just changing the word *little* to *giant* throughout the story, for example, creates a whole new story (and a lot of nonsense!). Changing the noun and verb also creates verbal fun:

Once there swam a little fish

The first sentence is a useful model for discussing how words seem to group together within long sentences:

Once there lived a little man
where a little river ran
and he had a little farm and little dairy O.

This kind of analysis helps the children know that long sentences are not merely made up of a lot of words, but rather, are made up of groups of words which fit together. This makes long sentences seem more manageable both for reading and writing.

The children may wish to keep this opening sentence on a card or in a notebook as a model story starter. This will encourage them to collect other worthwhile story starters.

7.–8. **Responding to typographical intrigue,** p. 92 and **Responding to art,** p. 94. It will be thought-provoking to invite the children into a discussion of how Ray Barber's decorative handlettering and John Rombola's decorative art go hand-in-hand to enhance the dance of syllables in this story. How different the over-all effect would be with heavy, undecorative type and with unadorned illustrations of appropriate objects.

Tatty Mae and Catty Mae

by Bill Martin Jr. illustrations by Aldren A. Watson

Two old cats lived on a houseboat.
One was named Tatty Mae.
The other was named Catty Mae.

Tatty Mae was a good fisherman.
Catty Mae was a good fisherman.
So they both were good fishermen.

Tatty Mae left her fish pole in the middle of the room.
Catty Mae left her fish pole in the middle of the room.
So they both left their fish poles in the middle of the room.

Tatty Mae left her fish net hanging on the doorknob. . . . .

Tatty Mae left her fish hooks in the bathtub. . . . .

Tatty Mae left her fish worms on the dresser. . . . .

Tatty Mae left her fishing coat on the chair. . . . .

Tatty Mae put her fishing boots on the bedpost. . . . .

Tatty Mae left her fishing cap on the pump handle. . . . .

One day Tatty Mae said to Catty Mae, "I declare, you're a litterbug!". .

Tatty Mae said, "I think we're both litterbugs!". . . . .

So Tatty Mae cleaned up and picked up and put away her litter. . . . . .

The next day Tatty Mae said, "Where is my fish pole?
Where is my fish net?
Where are my fish worms?"

The next day Catty Mae said, "Where is my fish pole? . . . .

So they both said, "Where is my fish pole? . . . .

Tatty Mae said, "Now, I'm all mixed up."
Catty Mae said, "Yes, the clean-up was a mix-up."
So they both said, "We'll never do it again."

And they didn't.

Children will quickly catch on to the repetitive structure in *Tatty Mae and Catty Mae*. Long before you finish the first reading, they will be listening for the first line in each episode so they can joyfully read right along with you. The children may wish to discuss their reactions to these lovable old cats who are much happier when things aren't too neat and clean, and they may wish to act out Tatty Mae and Catty Mae episodes before engaging in other of the suggested follow-up activities.

2. **Innovating on literary structure,** p. 77. and **Analyzing**
3. **literary structure,** p. 79. As the children discuss possible innovations on this story, they will probably also be discussing and analyzing their understanding of the literary structure. In addition to recognizing the repetitive pattern, you may wish to consider the notion that this is one of those stories where the main characters have a problem which must be solved. Won't it be fun when the children realize that Tatty Mae and Catty Mae solve their problem by refusing to recognize it as a problem!

5. **Analyzing sentence structure,** p. 86. Children will learn much about the position and function of words in sentences, as they transform and expand a basic sentence in this story.

Tatty Mae	*left*	*her long*	*fish worms*	*on the*	*dresser.*
	found	*slippery*		*in*	*bed.*
	swallowed			*under*	*rug.*

As they are discussing the ways words seem to cluster or fit together within sentences, you may also want to invite the children to consider how the sentences on each page of this story fit together. Each collection of sentences begins and ends, making way for a new collection. Discovering this fact can be an important step in knowing what paragraphs are all about. You might even want to rewrite *Tatty Mae and Catty Mae* in paragraph form on a reading chart.

6. **Analyzing word structure,** p. 90. This book offers many possibilities for worthwhile explorations into the ways words are put together. Compound words such as *houseboat* and *fishermen*, for example, might be the beginning of bulletin board lists of compound words. Comparisons of *fishermen* (one word) and *fishing coats* (two words) might lead to an investigation of other combinations of words in this and other stories which follow one or the other of these two patterns. The names *Tatty* and *Catty* might lead to lists of names which end in *y* and names which end in *ie*.

8. **Responding to art,** p. 94. Invite discussion of ways in which the artist portrayed the personalities of the two cats and also of the delightful details such as signs and birds. You may wish to discuss how carefully the type and art are arranged on the page to give plenty of space so that nothing looks cluttered even in a story about cluttering. Then invite the children to examine other arrangements of type and art in their books and to experiment with arrangements of their own.

I'm Going to Build a Supermarket One of These Days

by Helen Baten and Barbara von Molnar adapted by Bill Martin Jr.
with pictures by Papas

I'm going to build a supermarket one of these days,
called "LAND OF MILK AND HONEY,"
Where every shelf says HELP YOURSELF!
YOU DON'T NEED ANY MONEY!
I'm going to build a supermarket one of these days,
where adults are not admitted,
Where you roller-skate through the entrance gate,
and racing is permitted . . .

(continued on next page)

(continued from preceding page)

Where elephants wave the welcome flags...
Where kangaroos serve as shopping bags...
Where the piped-in music has a holiday sound...
Where you meet your friends on a merry-go-round...
Where the alphabet soup always spells your name...
Where you take time out for a baseball game...
Where a marshmallow bear is spinning cotton candy...
Where revolving shelves keep the ice cream handy . . .
Where coconut cakes wear a wreath of candles . . .
Where watermelon comes with juice-proof handles...
Where chickens lay Easter eggs, fancily dyed . . .
Where boxes of doughnuts are licorice tied . . .
Where you use the biggest grapefruit
    for a game of catch-the-bouncers...
Where you see the latest movies
    underneath the checkout counters . . .
Where you do target practice shooting holes in the cheese . . .
Where the fun never ends, stay as long as you please . . .
And when I build my supermarket one fine day,
I'll be sending you an airmail invitation . . .
. . . to come and shop with me, it's absolutely free . . .
    at my market with the SUPERreputation!

Children will enjoy this as a wish-fulfillment book as well as a book with a captivating jingle. What child hasn't wished for usual regulations to disappear as some familiar aspect of his life takes on fantasy dimensions?

1. **Reading joyfully from cover to cover,** p. 76. It may take several readings before the children are on their own in reading this book. Assigning chorus and solo choral reading parts will add pleasure to the children's repeated readings.

2. 3. **Innovating on literary structure,** p. 77 and **Analyzing literary structure,** p. 79. Children may decide to write innovations on the general theme of this story—telling about something imaginary they'd like to do "one of these days," without using the rhyme schemes of the original story. On the other hand, they may wish to analyze the rhyme schemes involved, noting the two different schemes and also the fact that certain lines have an internal rhyme scheme:

   Where you roller skate through the entrance gate,

   You may wish to give several days to this project, encouraging the children to put their innovations into book form adding covers, illustrations, title pages and other features of finished books. What fine additions to your reading table!

4. **Analyzing rhythmical structure,** p. 85. Just as there are two different rhyme schemes in this book, there are two definite rhythmical patterns. Clapping and comparing the two patterns will help the children verbalize that language does

have rhythmical patterns just as it has spelling patterns.

5. **Analyzing sentence structure,** p. 86. In addition to transforming the basic sentence in this story, children can be helped to appreciate the position and function of describing words in sentences by expanding the sentence.

beautiful
super *fine*
I'm going to build a ∧ supermarket one of these ∧ days.

6. **Analyzing word structure,** p. 90. The children can increase their knowledge and appreciation of compound words by experimenting with the word *supermarket*. How many words can they find in the dictionary which begin with *super*? How many can they think of which are not in the dictionary? How many can they invent?

8. **Responding to art,** p. 94. Here is a book that deserves picture-reading. Papas' joyous parade of cartoon-like drawings will evoke all sorts of language from the children.

Boys and girls, supposing this book were a comic book, can you use comic-book balloons to tell a story that goes with the pictures?

Do the artist's pictures give you any hints about how to paint or draw characters in action? Would you like to experiment with some of your own action pictures? Your own cartoon characters?

INSTANT READERS

LEVEL 2 Teacher's Guide

Follow-up activities for Level 2 books

PART 3

1. Reading joyfully from cover to cover

Immediately after reading one of the *Instant Readers* to the children, you will want to invite them to read the book "on their own." This can happen in a variety of ways:

(a) With a dependably structured book like *Old Devil Wind*, they will probably chime in long before you come to the last page. As their voices grow louder and louder, they will be proving to themselves and to you that they can successfully read the book.

(b) You may want to ask, *Children, would any of you like to try reading this book by yourselves?* If you have several copies of the book, so much the better. Give them out to the reaching hands, inviting the children to read on their own, read to one another, look over a friend's shoulder to read, and in other spontaneous ways to cement the fact that they can read the book.

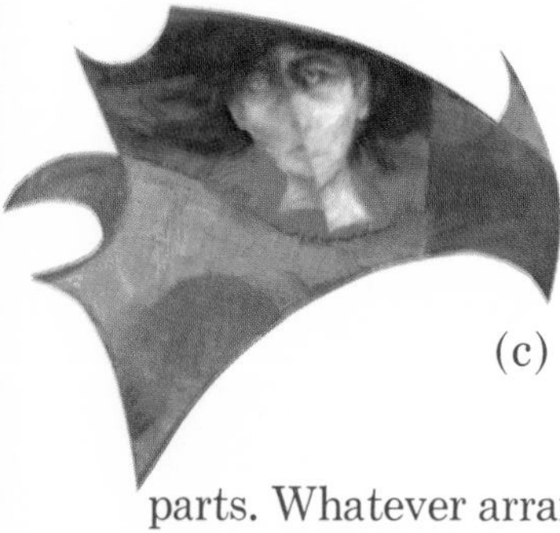

(c) Much of the children's read-aloud can turn into choral reading. Invite them to help you decide on various arrangements of chorus and solo parts. Whatever arrangements they decide upon, heart-warming dramatic and esthetic dimensions enter the classroom when choral reading takes the place of the semi-circle of children monotonously reading aloud one page at a time.

(d) Once the children have an *Instant Reader* firmly in their ears, their choral reading can take on the added dimensions of pantomime, dance and other forms of acting out.

(e) It can be useful to have a reading table or reading shelf where sure-fire books for the children's independent reading are kept. Then whenever the children have a free moment, they can select one of these special books to reinforce belief in themselves as readers. These "safe" books gradually become the bridge to the library and the children's wider world of independent reading.

2 □ Innovating on literary structure

When children borrow the underlying structure of a poem or story and hang their own ideas on that structure:

(a) they are having intuitive experiences with the fact that stories and poems do have underlying structures,

(b) they are building a bridge between the linguistic facts of their own worlds and the linguistic facts of the printed page.

The invitation to "write about anything you want to" may fall heavily on the ears of a child who doesn't own the basic language structures to give wings to what he wants to say. On the other hand, a child of seemingly meager vocabulary can latch onto a structure that comes in through his ears and deposits itself indelibly in his mind, and suddenly find his former meager vocabulary taking on new dimensions. The *Instant Readers* make it possible for children either of rich or meager vocabulary to find challenge in their new creations which come about as they innovate on the dependable structures found in these books.

Children, supposing you didn't want the story to be about a supermarket. What else might you want to build? (I'm Going to Build A Supermarket One of These Days.)

Children have been known to suggest *skyrocket, race car, classroom,* and many more.

And children, supposing you wanted to use the author's idea of having some of the lines rhyme.

It isn't important that the children borrow the author's exact rhyme scheme. Whatever plan for rhyming lines they decide upon, they are recognizing how easily certain words fall into place once a person is aware of the plan for making lines rhyme.

Can you imagine the innovations that are invited in *The Little Disaster?*

Once there lived a little man,
Where a little river ran,
And he had a little farm and little dairyO.

Once there lived a little ghost,
Who always liked to boast,
And he had a little sheet and box of magicO.

At some point, your room may be filled with reading charts made from the children's innovations. Exploit these charts for all they are worth, inviting children to read them, to identify new words they now recognize, to claim words for their wordcard collections.

Your reading table may come alive with 15 new books each time you read an *Instant Reader* and invite the children to borrow the structure and to adorn it with their own thoughts and language. What a wonderful source of material for the children's independent reading! Since all of the innovative books are built on structures which the children have already claimed in read-aloud times with the *Instant Readers*, the children will not only be able to read the new books more easily, but they will also be recognizing how useful a person's knowledge about underlying structure can be in helping him read.

3 □ Analyzing literary structure

When children realize that a story or poem has a plan back of it and when they recognize the specifics of that plan, they use this knowledge to predict much of the language they encounter in their reading. The *Instant Readers* give children five dependable kinds of literary structure to intake and analyze.

(a) *Repetitive structure.* As children listen to and read books like *Tatty Mae and Catty Mae,*

> *Two old cats lived on a houseboat.*
> *One was named Tatty Mae.*
> *The other was named Catty Mae.*

Tatty Mae was a good fisherman.
Catty Mae was a good fisherman.
So they both were good fishermen.

Tatty Mae left her fish pole
in the middle of the room.
Catty Mae left her fish pole
in the middle of the room.
So they both left their fish poles
in the middle of the room.

they soon catch on to the repetitive structure and find themselves able to read certain phrases and lines because they know from the pattern when the language will repeat.

(b) *Interlocking structure*. In contrast to the structure of *Tatty Mae and Catty Mae, Old Mother Middle Muddle* has episodes which do not simply repeat, but rather interlock with one another in an intriguing and dependable way:

Old Mother Middle Muddle
put down her knitting
and went to the kitchen to brew a cup of tea.

"O joy!" said the mouse,
"when Old Mother Middle Muddle
makes a cup of tea,
she's sure to have a cookie
and drop some crumbs for me."

"O joy!" said the cat,
"when the mouse comes out to eat the crumbs,
I'll pounce on him!"

"O joy!" said the dog,
"when the cat comes out to pounce on the mouse,
I'll bite her."

Once children have caught on to the interlocking nature of the plot structure, they will find themselves able to figure out much of the language in each subsequent episode.

(c) *Familiar cultural sequences.* A book like *A Spooky Story*, is hung around a repeated sentence pattern, cardinal number, and spooky vocabulary.

Out of the shadows,
out of the flum
comes one creeping cat.

Out of the shadows,
out of the flum
come two sweeping bats.

Once the children have read the first two episodes, part of their know-how in reading the rest of the book will come from their recognition that the author is increasing the number of creatures by one in each episode. Simply by living in our culture, they know how these ordinal numbers go and they will be able to read the corresponding words.

(d) *Cumulative structure.* Children who listen to *Old Devil Wind* will be depositing another useful literary structure in their linguistic storehouses.

> *One dark and stormy night*
> *Ghost floated out of the wall*
> *And he began to wail.*
>
> *Stool said, "Ghost, Ghost, why do you wail?"*
> *Ghost said, "It's a dark and stormy night*
> *and so I wail."*
> *And Stool said, "Then I shall thump."*
> *So Stool began to thump.*
>
> *Broom said, "Stool, why do you thump?"*
> *Stool said, "It's a dark and stormy night*
> *and Ghost wails and so I thump."*
> *Broom said, "Then I shall swish."*
> *So Broom began to swish.* (*Candle said, etc.*)

By the time the children have worked their way through the broom episode, they are able to predict the pattern of the story. They know that each new episode will carry everything that went in preceding episodes before adding the new happening. Because of this recognition of cumulative literary structure, the children are able to read much of the vocabulary in this book.

(e) *Rhyme scheme.* When children read

> *"Whistle, Mary, whistle,*
> *and you shall have a cow."*

"I can't whistle, Mother,
because I don't know how."

they have strong hunches about the way the author put his story together. Then when they read

"Whistle, Mary, whistle,
and you shall have a pig."
"I can't whistle, Mother,
because I'm not so big."

their hunches are confirmed: Mother will keep on asking Mary to whistle and Mary will keep on saying she can't, *because....*

One strong clue the children can count on in reading *Whistle, Mary, Whistle,* is the fact that it has an A B C B rhyme scheme. They will not use this sort of nomenclature in telling of their discovery, but they will expect the last line of each verse to rhyme with the second line, and they will use this expectation to figure out words which might otherwise be unknown.

After children have had the intuitive experience of reading a book partially because they are able to sense and use the clues given by the underlying structure, it can be useful to help them verbalize their intuitive experience and thus make it available as a decoding skill in future reading. This kind of verbalizing can best be triggered by questions which zero-in on the literary structure rather than the so-called story facts.

Children, when did you hunch that certain lines were going to be repeated again and again?

When did you first hunch that the author was going to use the numbers in their regular order beginning with 1?

When did you figure out that there were going to be rhyming words in this book?

When did you figure out where the rhyming words were going to be?

The children's responses to such questions will not be instantly forthcoming, especially in their early experiences with this kind of analyzing. Neither will they be precisely spoken nor all the same.

Well when the mother kept saying, "Whistle, Mary" and Mary kept saying, "I can't," I was pretty sure it would be this way all through the book.

When the word cow *at the end of the second line rhymed with the word* how *at the end of the last line in the first verse, I began wondering if it was going to be this way all through the book. Then when I read*

"Whistle, Mary, whistle,
and you shall have a goat."

my mind started thinking of words that would rhyme with goat.

When the broom explained to the candle all about the stool and all about the ghost, I was pretty sure they'd all just keep adding everything on.

One highly useful way for helping children verbalize their intuitive knowledge is to give them a verbal model for knowing what they know:

Isn't this exciting, children? Here you are figuring out the ways authors put their stories and poems together! Have you noticed, children, that the minute you catch on to the author's plan, your reading of a book gets easier?

4 □ Analyzing rhythmical structure

The *Instant Readers* are shot through with rhythm patterns which assist children in recalling sweeps of language and help them decode certain unknown words. By putting them in touch with their own rhythmic impulses, impressionable experiences with these kinds of books help children know that reading involves the entire body, not simply the eyes. For example, once the pattern is in their bloodstream, children will tend to chant, not merely say,

Once there lived a little man,
Where a little river ran,

And he had a little farm
and little dairyO!

And he had a little plough,
And a little dappled cow,

Which he often called
his pretty little FairyO!

In chanting, they will move to dancing and acting out if you but offer the invitation.

All of the time that they are engaging in this chanting and dancing, they are adding to their knowledge of how language works: it has a rhythm pattern just as surely as it has a spelling pattern. The more familiar children become with the rhythmical under-pinnings of language, the more enhanced are their reading and writing skills.

You will observe that after chanting and dancing *The Little Disaster*, children tend not to read the book, even when reading alone, in word-by-single-word fashion. The sentences will rise and fall in the natural sweeps of oral language. Moreover, you can help children generalize their first-hand experiences with rhythm into an expectation that rhythm will also be discovered in other stories they read and that the discovery will help them with their reading.

5. Analyzing sentence structure

Children need to make a go of spoken English sentences if they are to make a go of reading and writing the language. The sentence, not the word, is the basic linguistic unit. The most useful way of figuring out how sentences work is not to fill in countless workbook pages with missing periods and capital letters. Nor is it to memorize rules about how a sentence must have a complete thought. The best way to figure out how sentences work is to have one's head crammed with beautifully constructed sentences that have come in through the ear and are then available for experimentation in figuring out how they were put together.

The basic characteristic of sentences in English is the fact that certain words come in front of certain other words. Young children know this intuitively from learning to talk. At a very early age they may say, "Me hit you," using the incorrect pronoun, but they will not say, "Hit me you," placing the pronoun and verb in incorrect order.

The *Instant Readers* offer children a wide-ranging storehouse of sentence patterns. And even with young children, it is productive to engage in a gentle, non-didactic form of sentence analysis. After reading *King of the Mountain* and after the children have enjoyed reading it on their own several times, you might take a basic sentence pattern.

I'm the king of the mountain.

and invite the children to go through the book to see how many times the author used this same pattern, changing only one word.

I'm the king of the puddle.
pond.
lake.
river.
ocean. (*etc.*)

It will be interesting and useful for the children to verbalize the fact that once a person owns a few basic sentence patterns, he owns hundreds of sentences. Transforming sentences (substituting nouns for nouns, verbs for verbs, etc.) is the way a person changes his basic sentence patterns into new sentences. The children now might enjoy their own substitutions for naming words in the basic sentence:

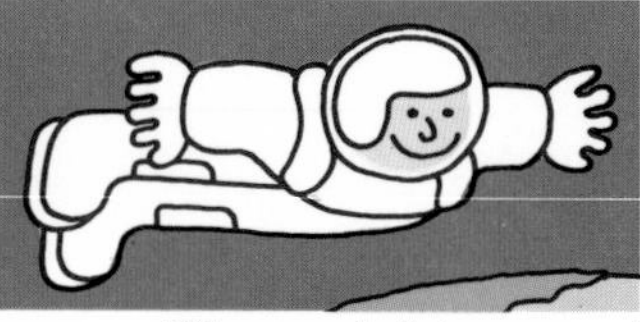

I'm the	*king*	*of the*	*mountain.*
	head		*government.*
	ruler		*people.*
	first	*in*	*line.*

They might even add substitutions for *I'm:*

I was
I will be
I should be

After the children have successfully transformed this basic sentence, you may wish to invite them to try their hands at *expanding* the sentence (adding describing words and phrases and clauses).

	defeated		*towering*		
	mighty		*magic*		
I'm the		*king of the*		*mountain.*	
					and I plan to reign forever.
					and I wish I had a queen.

As the children are engaging in sentence manipulations, you can carry on linguistically oriented conversations with them.

Children, isn't it interesting that the describing words come in front of the naming words they describe?

Don't be concerned if some children don't know exactly what you mean by *naming words* and *describing words* and don't be concerned if some children don't seem to know what you are saying. You can count on the fact that the children have intaken information about the position of words in English sentences on an intuitive level as they were learning to talk. Now as you verbalize this kind of information from time to time, they will gradually be able to recognize and verbalize their own intuitive knowledge.

You may even wish to help cement their appreciation of word-order in the English language by considering a poetic reversal in *City Song.* After reading

many windows
many floors
many people
many doors

etc. for 21 pages, the children suddenly encounter

families many . . .

Here is an opportunity to invite the children to state their preference regarding the position of the naming word and the describing word, reflecting upon the fact that although the poet frequently likes to reverse the order, for the most part English sentences have the describing word in front of the object it describes.

Once the children show enjoyment and satisfaction in sentence experimentation, search your *Instant Readers* for provocative sentences and have fun with them, knowing full well that the children will greatly improve their reading skills as they come to recognize how spoken and printed sentences work in the English language.

6 □ Analyzing word structure

Children spend much time looking for the exact features of a printed word that teachers guides require them to recognize. When it is time for beginning consonants, for example, a child is out of order if he notices the ending of a word. In contrast to this rigidly organized kind of word analysis, children need some time when they are invited into more spontaneous analyses of the printed page. Regardless of the features of printed words which are being studied at other times during the day and in other reading programs, children need invitations to make far-ranging and highly personal observations about patterns they see in printed words, knowing that all observations will be accepted and respected. Your open-ended questions will trigger such observations.

Children, what do you see interesting about the words on this page? (Accept any observations a child makes. If children identify beginnings and endings and middles of words, fine. If a child tells you the word *damage* looks like the storm in Westport, he may be telling you that he is a child who sees pictures rather than letter patterns when he looks at print. How exciting!)

The author of this book really likes to invent words (A Spooky Story). *Why do you suppose he spelled that word* flum *and not flume?* Won't it be in interesting to see if the children recognize that adding the letter *e* to the word would change the pronunciation of the letter *u?* Now might be a productive time for beginning a bulletin board list of words with and without that final *e*.

Let's take a look at that word castle (The Longest Journey in the World). *Can anyone remember other words ending in* le *that we have found in our* Instant Readers? (The children may quickly remember *whistle* from *Whistle, Mary, Whistle* and *little* from *The Little Disaster*. What a nice time to probe even further into the similarities and differences in these three words.)

What do you see interesting about the middles of some of the words on this page?

Who can find the word or words with the most syllables? (What a nice time for clapping the underlying rhythm of a page.)

Let's take a look at our book again and see how many times the first of two vowels is the one that is pronounced.

Hopefully, most of a child's word analysis activities will not be confused with the act of reading. Important though it can be for him to analyze words that are firmly entrenched in his linguistic storehouse through stories and poems, *his story books must not in his eyes symbolize endless drill.* Better to have a time in the day for word study in its own right. At such a time he can be analyzing word patterns found in his books if he so chooses, but he will not be interrupting the pleasures and linguistic wholeness of his reading.

From time to time you may wish to offer children word cards, phrase cards, sentence cards and punctuation cards for their personal collections of language reference materials. A shoe box serves handily as a container and what fun the children will have recreating on their desks, the conversation of Mary and her mother, adding their own innovations as they go. By the way, when children select words from the spooky stories included in the Level II *Instant Readers*, don't be surprised if they expect you or themselves to print these words in spooky writing. This is one impressive way to confirm their growing knowledge that the visual form of a word is important in reading.

7 □ Responding to typographical intrigue

Somewhere throughout the course of enjoying the *Instant Readers* with the children, you will want to take advantage of the fact that in many of these books the type swells, lurches, screams, whispers, undulates, turns somersaults, and even subsides in pictorial and narrative context. Having type behave in intriguing ways is not foreign to children. We adults have grown accustomed to schoolbooks where the same size and style of type move relentlessly from left to right, page after page, and it is easy to forget that today's children are encountering imaginative and flamboyant uses of type on TV, in magazine advertising and even on their cereal boxes.

Watch the children's faces as they follow the type lines when everything starts blowing away in *Old Devil Wind.*

AND THE BROOOOOMMMMMM..

AND THE STOOOOOOOOLLLLL..

AND THE CANDLEEEEEEEEE..

Notice how intently their eyes move with the type. In impressive ways these young children are learning the most basic characteristic of type–it moves from one place to another. The sad fact is, most of the early reading programs with their insistence on a rigid left-to-right non-varying pattern of print, actually cut children off from a fundamental cultural experience which tells children that print is after all a very versatile and exciting invention which to a large degree bends itself to the desires of the user. Rules about beginning on the left and moving to the right are not impressive invitations into the world of print. It is a child's recognition that type moves, a recognition which most easily comes from books where the movement is exaggerated, and his determination to figure out the plan back of the typographical puzzle that motivate a child to make a go of reading. Once he is caught up in the excitement of following the movement of type as he reads, he will himself come to the generalization that for the most part type does move from left to right.

You may wish to help the children verbalize their adventures with the type in the *Instant Readers.* How long was it before they discovered the extra vowels that exaggerated the movement when the wind blew things around in *Old Devil Wind?* Did they have any problem knowing which way the type went as the creatures moved out of the shadows and out of the flum in *A Spooky Story?*

You children are really getting to be fine detectives when it comes to following type on the page. Perhaps you would like to try writing your own stories with interesting arrangements of words.

For the psychological advantages as well as for pure enjoyment, from time to time write on the board familiar sentences in reverse direction, in scattered fields of letters, in upright rocketing, in straight downward plunges or in criss-cross fashion. Then watch the children delight as they put all of their linguistic skills into the decoding of the language. It is dramatic experiences of these kinds that stand children in good stead as they engage in the less exciting aspects of decoding. Children will work at identifying initial consonants or medial vowels or moving from left to right with more personal determination and pleasure when they see such activities as part of the larger and more exciting process of figuring out the puzzle of print.

8 □ Responding to art

Distinguished art is a hallmark of the Bill Martin books. Each of his series is a wide-ranging art gallery, exposing children to a wide variety of styles, media and design. The *Instant Reader* illustrations include woodcuts, collage, oil, watercolor, poster graphics, crayon, chalk. The range of technique includes cartoon, impressionistic, realistic, abstract, expressionistic. The designs vary from traditional use of type-space-art on a page to flamboyant interrelations that are startling in their unexpectedness. No child will remain passive to the visual aspects of the *Instant Readers.*

You and the children need not worry about the exact terminology as you discuss the art in a book. You can develop children's awarenesses of style and technique by asking:

Did you ever think a grown man would use crayons just as you do to illustrate a book? (Whistle Mary, Whistle)

Children, in Old Mother Middle Muddle, *the artist obviously didn't want an exact line around his paintings. How do you like his style compared with the kind of line the artist used in* King of the Mountain? (There is no right answer to this question. Making a choice is what is important.)

Have any of you children read other stories with illustrations that are something like the ones in I'm Going to Build a Supermarket One of These Days? (Recognizing the cartoon-style art in this book may invite a child to be curious about other styles as well as about his own preferences. This is what forming taste is all about.)

Let's see what the artist did to create a spooky mood in A Spooky Story. *Would you like to try painting to create a mood?*